HAND GRENADES

A HANDBOOK ON RIFLE AND HAND GRENADES

COMPILED AND ILLUSTRATED BY
MAJOR GRAHAM M. AINSLIE

1917

The Naval & Military Press Ltd

Published by the

The Naval & Military Press

in association with the Royal Armouries

Unit 10 Ridgewood Industrial Park,
Uckfield, East Sussex, TN22 5QE
Tel: +44 (0) 1825 749494
Fax: +44 (0) 1825 765701

MILITARY HISTORY AT YOUR FINGERTIPS
www.naval-military-press.com

ONLINE GENEALOGY RESEARCH
www.military-genealogy.com

ONLINE MILITARY CARTOGRAPHY
www.militarymaproom.com

*In reprinting in facsimile from the original, any imperfections are inevitably reproduced
and the quality may fall short of modern type and cartographic standards.*

PREFACE

THE purpose of this work is to assist students of grenade work in acquiring a rapid and complete knowledge of the subject. If the student will refer constantly to the illustrations, which are accurate drawings of grenades now in use, this book may help to elucidate many points which are inadequately treated in any existing work.

In compiling the book, the author has inserted only information absolutely necessary, and has arranged it so simply that a person with a very little previous knowledge of the subject may be able to grasp both the data given, and the principles, and methods herein explained and illustrated.

This book is the result of practical experience in the present war.

G. M. AINSLIE.

CONTENTS

HAND GRENADES

A GRENADE is a hollow ball, cylinder, or cube, made of metal or other material, which is filled with some explosive, and burst by means of a fuse, or on impact when it falls among an enemy. Until about the end of the seventeenth century trained soldiers called Grenadiers used grenades which were thrown by hand, but after that date they fell into disuse. In 1899–1900 at the siege of Mafeking they are said to have been used by the besieged, and also in the Russo-Japanese war. In the year 1914, however, the beginning of the great war produced new methods in the employment of infantry in the attack or defense of positions. It was proved that under many conditions infantry armed only with a rifle and bayonet found it impossible to press home an attack or hold a position against troops armed with grenades.

This weapon, handy to use and immensely destructive and demoralizing in its employment, has played a most important part in every successful operation carried out by British troops on the Western front. It has become one of the principal weapons not only in trench warfare, but in the attack and clearing of enemy positions, strong points, villages, and especially in house-to-house and cellar fighting.

NOTE. 1. In throwing all hand grenades an overarm action will be used, like a bowler when playing cricket.

2. Attached to all stick hand grenades are tapes or streamers a couple of feet long to enable them to fly head first, when thrown.

1

BRITISH GRENADES

There are two kinds of grenades:
    No. 1. Time grenades.
    No. 2. Percussion grenades.

No. 1 rely for ignition upon:
    (*a*) Some form of fuse lighter.
    (*b*) A length of time or safety fuse.
    (*c*) A detonator or exploder.

No 2 on:
    (*a*) Some form of percussion striking device.
    (*b*) A percussion cap.
    (*c*) A detonator.

For throwing purposes grenades as follows:
    1. Hand grenades.
    2. Stick hand grenades.
    3. Rifle grenades, fitted with firing rods 8 to 10 in.
        long.

GRENADE HAND NO. 1 or General Service

Type. Percussion stick grenade.
Weight. Two lb. complete.
Explosive. Lyddite.

Safety Device.
    1. Safety pin. Leather thong through eye of pin.
    2. Cord becket.
    3. Red indicator and words of directions on re-
        movable cap.

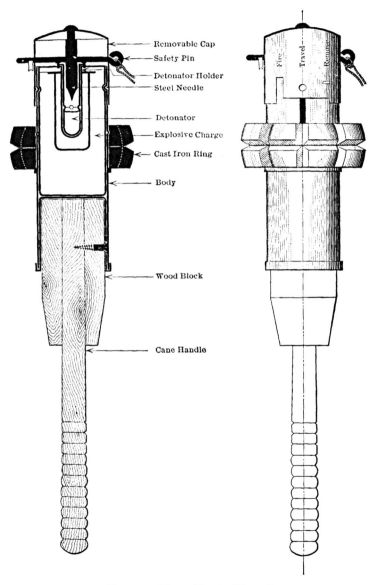

Removable Cap
Safety Pin
Detonator Holder
Steel Needle
Detonator
Explosive Charge
Cast Iron Ring
Body
Wood Block
Cane Handle

Fire Travel Remove

GRENADE HAND NO. 1, MARK 1.

Body.   Brass cylinder.
Striker.   Steel needle carried in removable cap.
Detonator.   Special detonator (see page 57.)
To prepare for use:

1. Turn word "remove" on cap to red indicator.
2. Take off removable cap.
3. Insert detonator.   Turn to left to secure.
4. Replace cap and turn to "travel."

To fire:

1. Turn cap to "fire."
2. Pull out leather thong from safety pin.   Remove cord becket.
3. Gather streamers palm right hand, holding grenade in left hand.
4. Holding grenade right hand, pull out safety pin with left hand.
5. Throw grenade.

Packing: Grenades are packed six in wooden box with tin containing ten special detonators.

Precautions: Care must be taken in act of throwing that grenade does not strike any object in rear of the thrower.

Always carry grenades at "travel."

GRENADE HAND NO. 2

Hales Hand or Mexican Grenade

Type.   Percussion stick grenade.
Weight.   One lb. complete.
Explosive.   Tonite.
Safety Device.   Safety pin.
Body.   Brass cylinder $4\frac{3}{4} \times 1\frac{1}{4}$ in. diameter.
Striker.   Brass needle pellet $1\frac{1}{2}$ in. long, conical head,

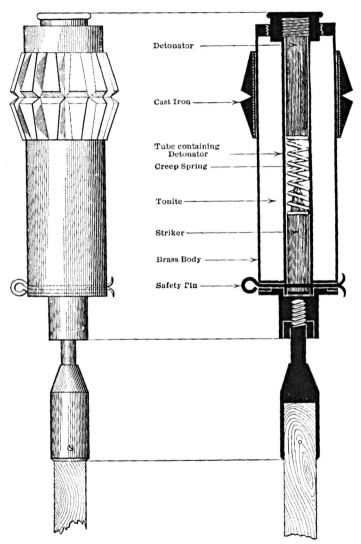

Detonator

Cast Iron

Tube containing
Detonator

Creep Spring

Tonite

Striker

Brass Body

Safety Pin

GRENADE HAND NO. 2. HALES GRENADE.

steel needle point, creep spring contained in brass base piece.

Detonator. Special No. 2.

To prepare for use:
1. Holding grenade head downwards, urscrew black ebonite, if needle pellet found secure.
2. Screw in detonator.

To fire:
1. Holding grenade in left hand, gather streamers palm of right hand.
2. Holding grenade right hand, pull out safety pin with left hand.
3. Throw grenade.

Packing. Grenades are packed ten in a wooden box, with tin containing ten No. 2 detonators.

Precautions. See Hand Grenade No. 1.

"GRENADE 303." SHORT RIFLE NO. 3
Hales Rifle Grenade

Type. Percussion.
Weight. One lb. 5 oz.
Explosive. Tonite.

Safety Device:
1. Safety pin.
2. Releasing collar.
3. Wind vane.
4. Retaining bolts.

Body. Serrated steel cylinder.

Striker. Brass fluted needle pellet $1\frac{1}{2}$ in. long, wasp waisted, conical head, steel needle point and creep spring, contained in brass base piece.

Detonator. Special No. 3 (see p. 57.)

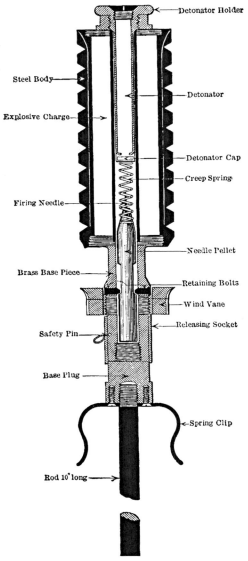

Detonator Holder

Steel Body

Explosive Charge

Detonator

Detonator Cap

Creep Spring

Firing Needle

Needle Pellet

Brass Base Piece

Retaining Bolts

Wind Vane

Releasing Socket

Safety Pin

Base Plug

Spring Clip

Rod 10″ long

"GRENADE 303." SHORT RIFLE NO. 3, MARK 1 (OR HALES RIFLE GRENADE).

To prepare for use:

1. Holding grenade head downwards, unscrew black ebonite block, if needle pellet found secure.
2. Screw in detonator.

To fire:

1. Oil rod and barrel of rifle.
2. Insert rod into barrel of rifle and work it up and down to ensure lubrication and to expel air.
3. Place special cartridge in chamber rifle and close bolt.
4. Pull out safety pin.
5. Pull down releasing collar.
6. Give wind vane $1\frac{1}{2}$ turns to left.
7. Fire the rifle.

Packing. Grenades packed twenty in wooden box in protecting tins with screw-off lids and four tins containing 20-in. special detonators, rifle, grenades and twenty-two special blank cartridges.

GRENADE HAND NO. 5. MARK I.

Mills Hand Grenade

Type.   Time $4\frac{1}{2}$ seconds.
Weight.   One and one-half lb.
Explosive.   Ammonal.

Safety Device:

1. Safety pin.
2. Striker lever.

Body.   Serrated oval cast iron.
Striker.   Steel rim firing.
Igniter.   Special, consisting of a separate unit.   Special

N.g. cap holder, N.G. rim firing percussion cap, $1\frac{3}{4}$-in. safety fuse and detonator.

To prepare for use:

1. Unscrew base plug.
2. Examine detonator and striker well for faults.

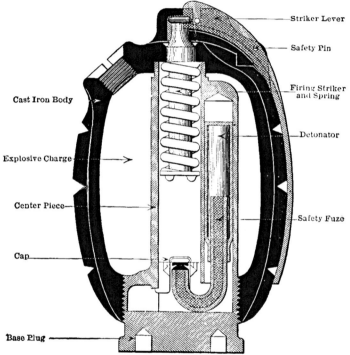

GRENADE HAND NO. 5, MARK 1 (OR MILLS GRENADE).

3. Insert special igniter.
4. Screw on base plug tightly by means of special key.

To fire:

1. Hold grenade in right hand, base plug up, the fingers holding the striker lever firmly against

the body of the grenade, the ring of the safety pin towards the left hand.

2. Pull out safety pin with the left hand, keeping the pressure on the striker lever.

3. Throw the grenade.

Packing. Grenades are packed twelve in wood box, with a tin containing twelve igniters.

Mills Rifle Grenade

Base plugs into which are screwed 8-in. rods are provided for this grenade to be fired from rifle, a special one being fitted to the rifle for this purpose.

GRENADES HAND NOS. 6 AND 7

R.L. or T.G. Grenades

Type. Time and friction.

Weight. No. 6 or light grenade, 1 lb. complete; No. 7, or heavy grenade, 1 lb. 13 oz.

Explosive.

Safety Device. Papier maché cap.

Body. Tin cylinder with rounded ends 4 in. long, $2\frac{1}{4}$ in. diameter.

Igniter. Special friction igniter, length of safety fuse, and service detonator combined.

To prepare for use:

1. Take off papier maché cap.

2. Take wooden plug out of detonator tube.

3. Insert friction lighter, turn to left and lock, clipping flange under studs.

4. Replace papier maché cap.

To fire:

  1. Remove papier maché cap.

  2. Hold grenade right hand, becket towards the wrist.

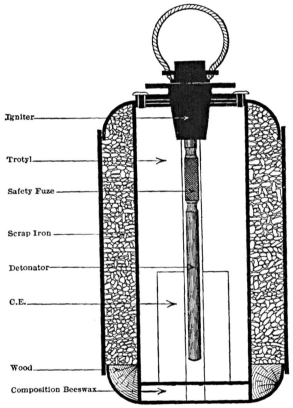

Igniter

Trotyl

Safety Fuze

Scrap Iron

Detonator

C.E.

Wood

Composition Beeswax

GRENADE No. 6, MARK 1.

  3. Pull out becket sharply with left hand.

  4. Throw grenade at once.

Packing. Grenades packed forty in wooden box. Four haversacks with four tins containing ten special igniters. These grenades should always be carried with papier maché caps on.

NOTE. The No. 6 grenade is an assault or demoralizing grenade.

GRENADE HAND NOS. 8 AND 9
Double Cylinder

Type. Time.

Weight. No. 8 light pattern, 1 lb. 6 oz. complete; No. 9, heavy pattern, 2 lb. complete.

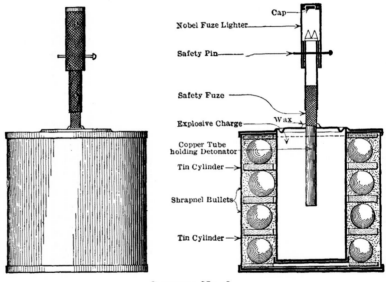

GRENADE No. 8.

Explosive.

Safety Device.

Body. Tin cylinder $2\frac{3}{4} \times 1\frac{1}{2}$ in. diameter, inside larger cylinder $3\frac{1}{4} \times 3$ in. diameter.

Igniter. Special Nobel lighter $1\frac{3}{4}$-in. safety fuse No. 8, VII detonator.

To prepare for use:

1. Crimp lighter on to fuse, insert fuse into detonator and crimp the latter on to fuse. Wax joints at lighter and detonator.
2. Insert igniter into detonator tube in inner cylinder.
3. Wax round joint where igniter enters grenade.
4. Wire fuse on to grenade.

To fire:

1. Hold grenade right hand, gripping bottom of Nobel lighter between thumb and finger.
2. Tear off tape and pull out safety pin.
3. Press down outer tube of N. lighter, turn sharply to R. or L.
4. Throw grenade at once.

NOTE. The heavy pattern grenade has more shrapnel and less explosive than the light pattern grenade.

GRENADE HAND NO. 12

Hairbrush or Box Pattern Grenade

Type. Time, or land mine.

Weight. Three lb. complete.

Explosive. Ammonal or guncotton.

Safety Device. Safety pin.

Body. Tin box $3 \times 5 \times 2$ in. A grooved cast-iron plate, $\frac{1}{4}$ in., forms the front side.

Igniter. Special brass tube consisting of spring and striker held in place by safety pin. Cap and fuse and detonator or Nobel lighter, fuse and detonator.

To prepare for use. See Nos. 8 and 9 grenades.

To fire. See Nos. 8 and 9 grenades.

NOTE. This grenade is now used as a land mine.

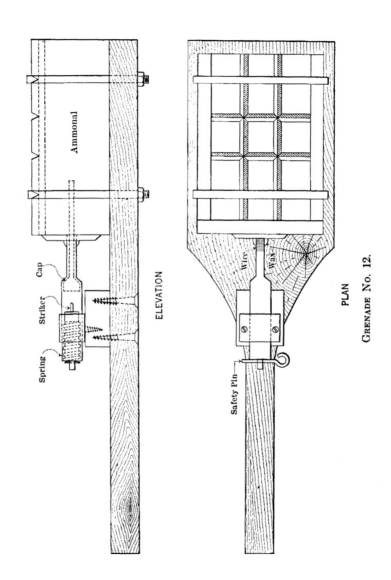

ELEVATION

Ammonal

Cap

Striker

Spring

PLAN

Wire

Wax

Safety Pin

GRENADE No. 12.

BATTYE GRENADE

Type. Time.

Weight. One lb. 2 oz. complete.

Explosive. Ammonal guncotton, $1\frac{1}{2}$ oz.

Safety Device. Safety pin in Nobel lighter.

Body. Cast-iron cylinder, 3×2 in. diameter, one end solid.

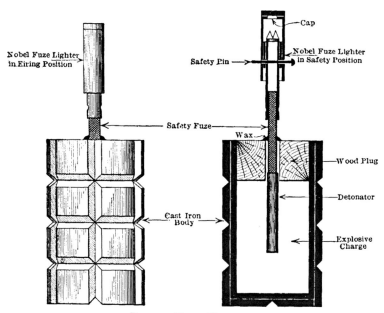

BATTYE HAND GRENADE.

Igniter. Nobel lighter, $1\frac{3}{4}$-in. fuse, No. 8 M.K. VII detonator.

To prepare for use. See Grenade Hand No. 8.

To fire. See Grenade Hand No. 8.

Packing. Grenades packed thirty in wooden box arranged with removable wooden partitions which rest on top of the grenades, to prevent lid coming in contact with the end of the igniters.

PITCHER HAND GRENADE

Type. Time.
Weight. One and one-half lb.
Explosive. Ammonal.
Safety Device.

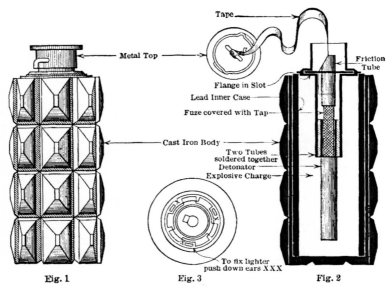

PITCHER HAND GRENADE.

Body. Cast-iron cylinder $4 \times 1\frac{7}{8}$ in. diameter, one end solid.

Igniter. Special.

This grenade is not likely to be reissued. The igniter is described in the Training and Employment of Grenadiers issued by General H. Q., October, 1915.

OVAL GRENADE

Type. Time.

Weight. One lb. 2 oz. complete.

Explosive. Ammonal.

Safety Device. Brock lighter. (See Patent Lighters, p. 58.)

Body. $\frac{3}{16}$-in. cast-iron, egg-shaped, $3\frac{1}{2}$ in. long $\times 2\frac{1}{4}$ in. diameter at middle.

Igniter. Brock lighter, $1\frac{3}{4}$ in. fuse, No. 8 M.K. VII detonator.

To prepare for use. See Hand Grenade No. 8.

To fire:

1. Hold grenade right hand.
2. Pull off waterproof paper on Brock lighter with left hand.
3. Strike lighter against brassard carried on left arm for this purpose.
4. Throw grenade at once.

Precautions. The waterproof paper must not be removed before throwing, as composition may get damp, or grenade accidentally lighted.

BALL GRENADE

Type. Time.

Weight. One lb. $11\frac{1}{2}$ oz. complete.

Explosive. Ammonal, $5\frac{1}{2}$ oz.

Safety Device. Safety pin in Nobel lighter. (See Patent Lighter.)

Body. Cast-iron sphere, 3 in. diameter.

Igniter. Nobel lighter, $1\frac{3}{4}$-in. fuse, No. 8 M.K. VII detonator.

To Prepare for Use. See Hand Grenade No. 8.
To Fire. See Hand Grenade No. 8.

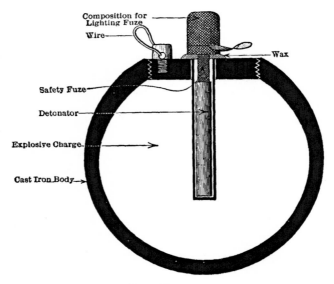

BALL GRENADE.

NEWTON HAND GRENADE

Type. Time, $4\frac{1}{2}$ seconds.
Weight. One lb. 5 oz.
Explosive. Ammonal.
Safety Device. Special split tin disc over N.G. percussion cap.
Body. Cast-iron, pear-shaped.
Striker. Contained in special striker cap.
Igniter. Sawed off .303-in. blank cartridge, $1\frac{3}{4}$-in. safety fuse, detonator.

To Prepare for Use:
    1. Remove striker cap.
    2. Insert igniter.

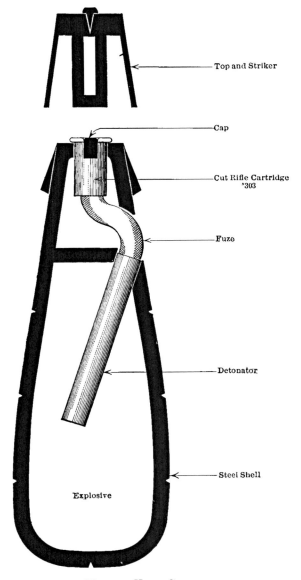

Top and Striker

Cap

Cut Rifle Cartridge
'303

Fuze

Detonator

Steel Shell

Explosive

NEWTON HAND GRENADE.

3. Slip on safety device.
4. Replace striker cap.

To Fire:

1. Hold grenade in right hand, narrow end downwards.
2. Bring striker cap down a sharp blow on brassard carried on left thigh for that purpose, or upon some hard surface.
3. Throw grenade at once.

NEWTON RIFLE GRENADE

Type. Percussion.
Weight. One lb.
Explosive. Ammonal.
Safety Device. Newton Hand.
Body. Cast-iron conical.
Striker. Newton Hand.
Detonator. Commercial.

To Prepare for Use:

1. Remove striker cap.
2. Insert detonator.
3. Slip on safety device.
4. Replace striker cap.

To Fire:

1. Oil 10-in. rod and barrel of rifle.
2. Work rod up and down to insure lubrication and to expel air.
3. Place special blank cartridge in chamber of rifle and close bolt.
4. Fire the rifle.

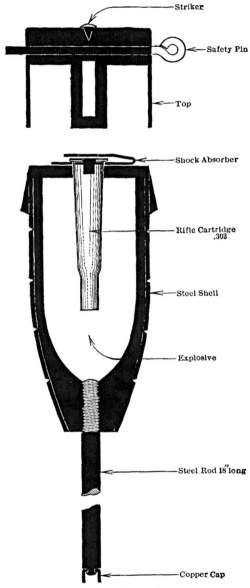

NEWTON RIFLE GRENADE.

HAND GRENADE NO. 19

Type. Percussion stick grenade.
Weight. One and three-quarter lb.
Explosive. Ammonal.

Safety Device:

1. Safety pin.
2. Shearing wire.

Body. Oval, cast-iron.
Striker. Mushroom-topped brass.
Detonator. Special long commercial.
Igniter. (Sawed off) 380-in. blank cartridge.

To Prepare for Use:

1. Unscrew brass striker holder.
2. Insert detonator.
3. Screw on brass striker holder.

To Fire:

1. Unwind streamer at end of handle.
2. Hold grenade in left hand, gather up streamers palm of right hand.
3. Holding grenade in right hand, take out safety pin with left hand.
4. Throw grenade.

Packing. Grenades are packed twelve in a wooden box, also a tin containing twelve special detonators.

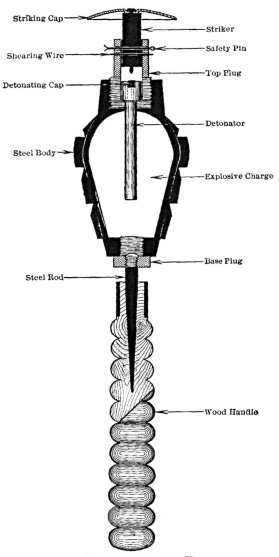

GRENADE NO. 19.   HAND.

RIFLE GRENADE NO. 20

Improved Hales Rifle Grenade

Type. Percussion.
Weight. One lb. 8 oz.
Explosive. Tonite.

Safety Device:

1. Safety pin.
2. Releasing collar.
3. Retaining bolts.

Body. Steel cylinder.
Striker. Same as No. 3 Rifle Grenade (see p. 7).
Detonator. Special No. 3 (see p. 7.)

To Prepare for Use:
1 and 2. See No 3 Rifle Grenade (see p. 7).

To Fire:

1, 2, 3, and 4 same as No. 3 rifle grenade, see p. 7, Fire Rifle.

Packing. Grenades packed twenty in wooden box, four tins containing five each "special detonators rifle grenade," and 22 special blank cartridges.

Precautions. See all stick hand grenades.

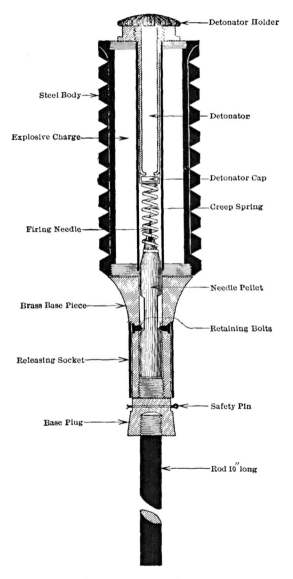

RIFLE GRENADE NO. 20.

DIVISIONAL GRENADE ESTABLISHMENT AND CHAINS OF AUTHORITY

Divisional Grenade Officer and Instructional Staff for Grenade, Stokes Gun, Trench Mortar Schools.

Brigade Grenadiers:

1. Sergt. Major.
1. Q.M.S.
4. Sergt. Instructors.
4. Grenade platoons, per battalion in brigade.

Battalion Grenadiers of Grenade Platoon:

1. Grenade officer.
1. Sergt. Instructor.
4. N.C.O.'s and 40 men.
1. Cook.
1. Officers' servant.

Total, 48 all ranks.

Company Grenadiers:

1. N.C.O. and 10 men per platoon.
4. N.C.O.'s and 40 men per company.
16. N.C.O's and 160 men per battalion.

Total grenadiers per battalion, 224 all ranks.

Total grenadiers per brigade, 896 company and battalion grenadiers.

Total grenadiers per division, 2688 company and battalion grenadiers.

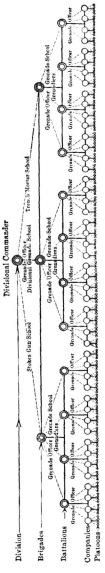

DIVISIONAL GRENADIER ESTABLISHMENT SHOWING CHAIN OF RESPONSIBILITY.

COMPOSITION OF A GRENADE SQUAD

In Line	In Single File
No. 1. Bayonet man.	No. 1. Bayonet man.
No. 2. Bayonet man.	No. 2. Bayonet man.
No. 3. First thrower.	No. 3. First thrower.
No. 4. Second thrower.	No. 6. First carrier.
No. 5. N.C.O. or Leader.	No. 5. N.C.O. or Leader.
No. 6. First carrier.	No. 4. Second thrower.
No. 7. Second carrier.	No. 7. Second carrier.
No. 8. Spare man.	No. 8. Spare man.
No. 9. Spare man or sniper.	No. 9. Spare man or sniper.

Duties of Above. *Nos. 1 and 2 Bayonet Man.* 1.
Clearing of a Trench to a Flank. They are the body-
guard for the thrower and carrier and must always protect them under any conditions and at all costs.

NOTE. The latter are not armed against attack at
close quarters. The bayonet men work in advance of
the thrower and carrier of their squads. They act as
trench scouts; that is, they instruct their thrower and
carrier how the trench runs and where the dug-outs and
side trenches will be met. They will carry their rifles
with bayonets fixed, loaded, magazine full. No. 3 and 6
bomb and clear all dug-outs on the way down the trench.
The first man throws the bomb, the bayonet man enters
the dug-out and completes its work. At the junctions of
communication trenches and side trenches they act as
trench sentries and observers until relieved by the squads
in rear. If necessity arises they assist the thrower by
throwing bombs.

2. *Frontal Attack against Enemy Positions.* They will
be in line with, not in advance of the thrower and
carrier and will protect them while throwing by snap

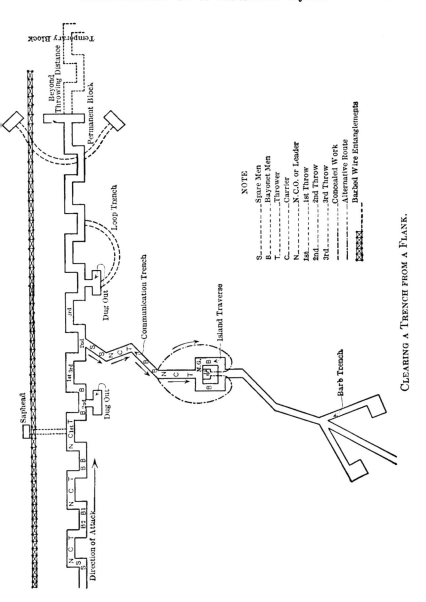

CLEARING A TRENCH FROM A FLANK.

NOTE

S --------- Spare Men
B --------- Bayonet Men
T --------- Thrower
C --------- Carrier
N --------- N.C.O. or Leader
1st --------- 1st Throw
2nd --------- 2nd Throw
3rd --------- 3rd Throw
-·-·-·- Concealed Work
--------- Alternative Route
⬛⬛⬛--- Barbed Wire Entanglements

shooting, or with their bayonets against assault, or a
sudden rush by the enemy when at close quarters.

3. *Street Fighting and Village Cleaning.* They will
keep down enemy rifle fire by snap shooting, so as to
enable the thrower to work close enough to his objective
to throw grenades, and when these have burst, will
go forward and complete their work.

No. 3. First Thrower. He throws grenades according
to the directions given him by his leader or by his bayonet
men. He is a picked man, steady under fire and chosen
for his accuracy and length in throwing.

No. 4. The Carrier. He follows close enough in
rear of the throwers to keep them supplied with grenades, but must be careful not to crowd them or im-
pede the throwing. He will be prepared to instantly
take up the duties of the thrower should he become a
casualty.

No. 5. N.C.O. or Leader. He is responsible for his
squad and the proper carrying out of the duties given to
the squad. He will inspect each man before an attack
and see that he has his complete equipment and that
he knows the general idea and direction of the attack
and the final objective of his squad. He will be responsible for the maintenance of supplies of grenades through
his squad to the thrower, and will supervise the auto-
matic filling up of casualties in his squad by men from the
squads in the rear. He will indicate the position and
progress of his squad in the attack to supporting troops,
etc., by means of flags or other signals by day and by
colored flares by night.

Nos. 6, 7, 8 and 9. Their duties are the same as
Nos. 1, 2, 3 and 4, and are to be considered primarily
as carriers until otherwise employed.

No. 10. Spare Man. He will act, if necessity arises, as
leader of his section, to clear side trenches, etc., and will

instantly take over the duties of No. 5 should he become a casualty.

No. 11. Sniper. He will act as a sniper by day and a connecting file by night, between his own squad and the squad of troops in rear.

NOTE. Every man in the grenade squad should be trained to fill the position of any other in the squad.

Explanation of Chart No. A2. The position occupied by grenadiers in an attacking squad has this main point in consideration.

The safety and local protection of each individual in the squad; care should be taken that as far as possible each man has a solid corner of the trench close to him, which he can use as a protection against the bursting effect of enemy grenades, by quickly advancing or retiring around the corner.

The bayonet men are in advance of the thrower, close enough to protect him, and not too far in front as to be in danger of being bombed by him.

The thrower—the actual means of attack—is ·protected in front by the traverse and in the rear by the corner of the parados. The carrier is close behind the thrower and is protected by two corners. The N.C.O. or leader is where he can best watch the flight of the grenades thrown by the throwers, and is also equally well protected.

Method of Advance. It is usually the endeavor to bomb and clear three bays at a time in advance of the bayonet men. The N.C.O. reports the throwing by the word "Mark," to indicate a burst in the required bay. On the third mark having been registered, the N.C.O. gives the order, "Bayonet men report." They immediately advance up the trench to the last bay cleared and report back after examination either "All clear" or "Enemy holding," whereupon the N.C.O. gives the order "Advance," or directs the thrower to bomb the last bay again. This means of advance is continued until the objective is gained.

Island Traverse. The two methods of attack are employed as shown on the chart. It is imperative that the attack must not be allowed to be held up, and should it be found impossible to advance down the trench itself, owing to enfilade fire, the attack must be immediately launched outside the trench, so as to attack the traverse from the rear, in the case of a daylight attack.

Precautions. Care must be taken, especially by the bayonet men in their advance through the trench, that enemy concealed trenches, dug-outs, etc., are not left undiscovered. The sides of trenches and the walls and floors of dug-outs should be carefully examined for concealed entrances or exits.

FRONTAL ATTACK

IN CONJUNCTION WITH INFANTRY

The Preparation Before an Attack. The following details must be carefully considered:

(a) The study of operation orders.

(b) The linking up of observations gained from the

1. Study of existing trenches and aeroplane maps of enemy positions.
2. The personal reconnaissance of the topographical features of the ground to be covered in the advance.

(c) The detailing of squads to their special objectives and the arranging for work, carrying wire and demolishing parties for permanent blocks at the final objectives.

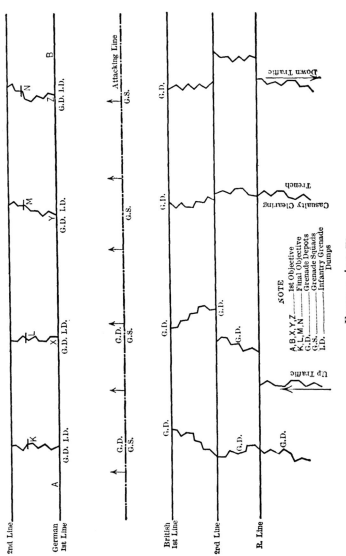

FRONTAL ATTACK.

NOTE

A,B,X,Y,Z .... 1st Objective
K,L,M,N .... Final Objective
G.D. .... Grenade Depots
G.S. .... Grenade Squads
I.D. .... Infantry Grenade Dumps

(*d*) The kind of grenades to be used with a view to facilitating the carrying of same.

(*e*) Carrying parties must be told off to insure supplies of grenades reaching the throwers.

(*f*) Grenade depots must be built, sign boards arranged for, and clearly marked "Grenade Depot" not only in our own system of trenches, but also the positions told off beforehand where they are to be established in the enemy trenches, or in **No Man's Land** immediately previous to the attack.

(*g*) Responsible officers and N.C.O's should be told off to look after the grenade depots and supply of grenades.

(*h*) The position for infantry grenade dumps must be selected and clearly explained to all units taking part in the attack, and special parties told off to collect at these points and carry grenades to nearest depots.

(*i*) A traffic system should be arranged and all men must be acquainted with it, and the trenches or lines of travel clearly marked "up traffic," etc.

The Advance.

    1. In line with infantry.

    2. In advance of infantry.

No. 1 is the method adopted in daylight attack, the advance not being covered by gas or smoke clouds.

No. 2 is method adopted in night attack and when weather conditions or topographical features of ground covered in the advance allow it.

Attacking squads are allotted positions in lines of infantry immediately opposite their first objectives, and on reaching these positions should immediately commence bombing and clearing the trenches towards their final objectives. In the case of No. 1 the infantry clear the main trench, but special grenade parties may be told off to assist the infantry in this work, especially when strong points occur in the enemy position.

It is most important that all infantry taking part in an attack should be previously supplied with grenades and this must be considered the first source of supply. Positions designated as infantry grenade dumping positions should be chosen and known to the infantry at which they dump their grenades in their advance on the enemy positions. These positions should be close to the position to be captured and held.

In order to hold positions captured from the enemy it is imperative that grenade storming parties hold their final objectives at all costs, and until the positions to be permanently held have been consolidated.

TRENCH STORMING PARTIES

Trench storming parties should kill or drive back the hostile occupants of a trench as quickly as possible, clear as much of the enemy trench as has been ordered, and then hold the portion cleared with as small loss as possible to themselves. It must be remembered that in trench clearing, and especially in deep and narrow trenches, only the head of the attacking party can directly kill, and seldom more than one man can throw at a time. Therefore it is essential that a constant supply of grenades reaches the thrower and that the places of casualties are automatically filled by reinforcements. Men must be trained until they can do this either by day or at night time.

Advance. Movement is rapid until contact with the enemy is obtained. Once contact is established it must be maintained and pressed home. A retreating enemy must be given no time to re-establish a defensive attitude, corners must be worked carefully and bays and straight pieces of trench rushed. The bayonet men will complete the work of the grenades and see that the carrier and thrower will meet with no opposition on their way to new throwing position. The effect of a grenade bursting in a confined space like a trench is tremendous, and though it may not kill it will stun or shock the hostile occupants, and if the bayonet men follow up rapidly they will meet with very little resistance.

Casualties. Every man must be trained to take up the duties of any other man in his squad. They do not necessarily keep to their own squads; the squads in rear of the attacking squad may be looked on as a reserve squad for the one in front. Thus, Casualty first squad. The thrower No. 3 is reinforced by the first thrower of the second squad, and so on.

Side Trenches. When a side trench is met with, the leading squad will go up and clear it. The second half will remain at the junction until first returns, then the second squad will continue advance in original direction of the attack.

Blocking and Barricades. For blocking captured trenches, etc., see Manual of Field Engineering, Wire Entanglements, Hurdles, etc.

FOREIGN GRENADES. FRENCH

The description of British and German grenades apply also to those grenades used by the French army.   They are:

1. Three kinds of petards.
2. Pear-shaped percussion grenade hand.
3. The "Besozzi" grenade.

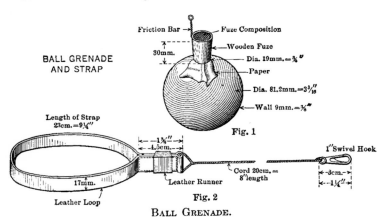

BALL GRENADE AND STRAP

Friction Bar → — Fuze Composition

—Wooden Fuze

30mm.

— Dia. 19mm. = ¾″

—Paper

— Dia. 81.2mm. = 3³⁄₁₆″

← Wall 9mm. = ⅜″

Fig. 1

Length of Strap
23cm. = 9¼″

—1⅛″—
—4.5cm.—

1″ Swivel Hook

17mm.

Leather Runner

Cord 20cm. =
8″ length

←-3cm.-→
←-1¼″-→

Leather Loop

Fig. 2

BALL GRENADE.

1. BALL GRENADE OR FORTRESS GRENADE
Description

Igniter.   Friction tube with wire pull let into wooden fuse.

Safety Devices:
1. The fuse is carried separate.
2. The plug is covered with paper.
3. The wire pull is bent to prevent a direct pull of the fuse.

To Use.   See German spherical Grenade, p. 43.

2. PEAR-SHAPED GRENADE—Percussion

Description

Igniter. A copper tube containing striker, creep spring and detonator.

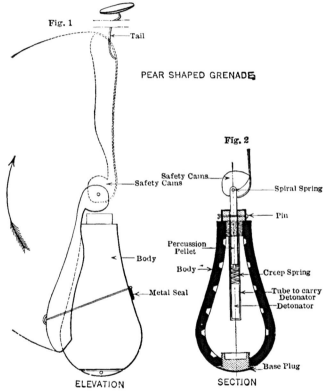

Fig. 1

Tail

PEAR SHAPED GRENADE

Fig. 2

Safety Cams

Safety Cams

Spiral Spring

Pin

Percussion Pellet

Body

Body

Creep Spring

Metal Seal

Tube to carry Detonator

Detonator

Base Plug

ELEVATION

SECTION

PEAR-SHAPED GRENADE.

Safety Devices:

1. The cams lever secures striker while the lever is held in place against body of grenade.
2. The strong loop which holds lever against body of grenade and is fastened by a metal seal.

How to Use:

1. **This grenade is always " alive."**
2. Holding grenade in right hand, neck towards the wrist, the lever against the palm of the hand.
3. Pull off the metal seal with left hand.
4. Throw the grenade.

NOTE. This grenade must be carefully handled; it is carried and packed "alive."

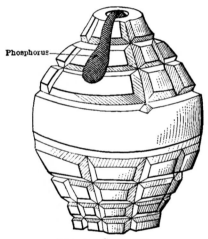

Phosphorus—

BESOZZI GRENADE.

3. BESOZZI GRENADE

Description

Igniter:

1. Time fuse with projects from the grenade.
2. Red phosphorus tipping to fuse.
3. Detonator.

Safety Devices:

1. The grenades are packed in waterproof paper.

To Use:

1. Holding grenade in the right hand, fuse upwards.
2. Strike the phosphorus tip with a downwards motion of the left hand, with the striking box.
3. Throw the grenade at once.

NOTES.   1. Fuse burns 5 seconds.

2. These grenades are always carried alive.

3. A special ring or striking box is provided to light the fuse.

Foreign Hair Brush Grenades. They are similar to the British No. 12 Hand Grenades.

GERMAN GRENADES

There are two types:

No. 1. Service grenades.

No. 2. Improvised or home-made grenades.

These are again divided into two classes:

A. Those that depend for their effect upon fragmentation on detonation.

B. Those that depend for their effect upon the shock of detonation only.

The type **B** is more commonly met with than type **A**. Ignition is by time or percussion. The time of fuses about six seconds burning.

Precautions. When handling foreign grenades care should always be taken and the following rules should be enforced:

1. Only skilled grenadiers should be allowed to examine and handle any grenades found.

2. Grenade depots when discovered should be immediately reported to the nearest grenadier.

3. Foreign time grenades should be thrown as soon as the lighting device has been started.

Description of German Grenades

As the means of firing a grenade will be immediately apparent to the skilled grenadier on seeing the grenade, the following information only is of importance to the unskilled grenadier:

1. How to make the grenade safe.

2. How to make the grenade alive.

3. How to use the grenade against the enemy.

SPHERICAL GRENADE

1. How to Make Safe:

1. Screw out the special lighter, taking care not to pull the wire.

2. How to Make the Grenade Alive:

1. Screw in the special lighter.
2. Remove the oiled paper, straighten the wire.

3. How to Use the Grenade:

1. Put on wrist strap.
2. Hold grenade in the right hand, igniter towards the wrist.
3. Hook the swivel of the wrist strap on to the wire pull of the grenade.
4. Throw the grenade at once.

NOTE. Use time of fuse burning, seven seconds, but another lighter which burns for five seconds—painted red—is also provided.

STICK CYLINDER GRENADE

See p. 44.
1. How to Make Safe:

1. Remove the handle and base plug by raising turned down edge of the cylinder carefully.
2. Empty contents of cylinder.

2. How to Make the Grenade Alive:

1. See the British Grenades Hand No. 12.

3. How to Use the Grenade:

1. Pull out safety pin.
2. Throw the grenade at once.

Note. Fuse about 2 in. long. Burns about six seconds.

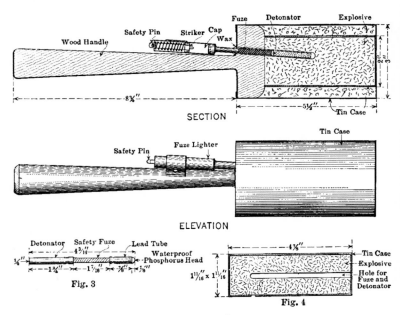

STICK CYLINDER GRENADE.

SMALL STICK CYLINDER GRENADE

See p. 45.

1. How to Make Safe:

1. Take out igniter.

2. How to Make the Grenade Alive:

1. Take out wooden plug and insert the igniter.
2. Tear off paper cover from the lighter.

3. How to Use the Grenade:

1. Holding grenade in right hand, rub the match head on the side of a match box, etc.
2. Throw the grenade at once.

NOTE.   Time fuse burns about six seconds.

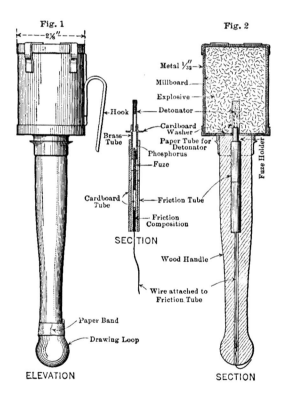

Fig. 1

2⅜″

←Hook

Brass Tube

Cardboard Tube

SECTION

Cardboard Tube

Paper Band

Drawing Loop

ELEVATION

Fig. 2

Metal ¹⁄₃₂″→

Millboard

Explosive

Detonator

Cardboard Washer

Paper Tube for Detonator

Phosphorus

Fuze

Friction Tube

Friction Composition

Fuze Holder

Wood Handle

Wire attached to Friction Tube

SECTION

CYLINDRICAL GRENADE

See p. 44.

Regulation Type

1. How to Make Safe:

1. Unfasten clips which hold lid of cylinder.
2. Remove cardboard cylinder containing explosive.
3. Insert hand and withdraw detonator from brass tube at end of handle.

2. How to Make Alive:

1. If drawing loop is attached to handle by paper band, unscrew handle and insert special detonator into brass tube at end of handle and refix handle.

3. How to Use the Grenade:

1. Holding grenade in right hand.
2. Pull loop sharply with left hand.
3. Throw the grenade at once.

NOTE. Time fuse burns is stamped on handle $5\frac{1}{2}$ or seven seconds. Care must be taken when grenade is found without the pull loop, in case it has been fixed to light on unscrewing handle.

OYSTER SHELL OR DISC HAND GRENADE

See p. 47.

1. How to Make Safe:

1. If safety pin is in place, unscrew cap marked **S**.
2. Remove detonator.

NOTE. If safety pins and safety tubes are not in place, the above must be done without disturbing the grenade.

2. How to Make Alive:

1. This grenade is packed alive.

3. How to Use the Grenade:

1. Holding grenade in right hand, safety pin upwards, pull out safety pin with left hand.
2. Pull off the cap of the safety tube.

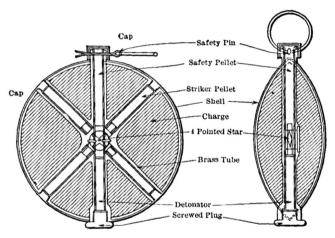

Cap

Safety Pin

Safety Pellet

Striker Pellet

Shell

Charge

4 Pointed Star

Brass Tube

Cap

Detonator

Screwed Plug

DISK HAND GRENADE.

3. Holding the grenade with the first or middle finger on top of the safety tube and the ball of the thumb over the cap marked **B**.
4. Throw the grenade with its edge vertical.

NOTE. A low or horizontal throw may cause a failure.

PARACHUTE GRENADE

See p. 48.

1. How to Make Safe:

1. Unscrew the plug in the head.
2. Withdraw the detonator.

2. How to Make Alive:

1. Unscrew the plug and insert detonator, fulminate downwards.
2. Screw the plug and tear off band holding parachute.

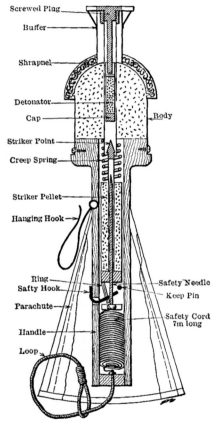

PARACHUTE GRENADE.

3. How to Use the Grenade:

1. Hold loop of cord firmly with fingers of right hand.

2. Tear out plug from handle and unwind a short length of the cord.

3. Holding the grenade in right hand, the first and second fingers firmly in the loop of the cord.

4. Throw the grenade to a height of at least 3 to 4 yards.

NOTE. This grenade requires considerable practice.

RIFLE GRENADES

See p. 50.

1913 and 1914

1. How to Make Safe:

1. Unscrew igniter plug in the head of 1913 grenade. Unscrew fuse from the body of 1914 grenade.

2. How to Make Alive:

1. Screw igniter into head of 1913 grenade. Screw fuse into body of 1914 grenade.

3. How to Use the Grenade:

1. Follow out custom of firing British Rifle Grenades.

NOTE. Only a German rifle can be used, and more care in handling the grenade before firing must be taken than with the British grenades, they are liable to become "alive" if dropped on to the tail rods.

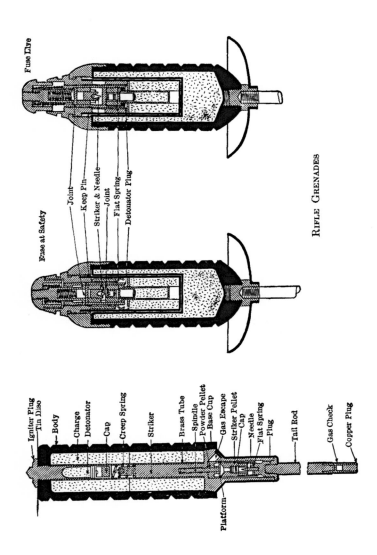

RIFLE GRENADES

EXPLOSIVES USED IN GRENADES

Explosives are divided into two classes:
1. Low explosives.
2. High explosives.

To the first group belong all propellant explosives, i.e., all powders, such as gunpowder and smokeless powders used in firearms.

To the second group belong:

(a) All explosives used in shells, torpedoes, grenades, demolitions, etc.

(b) Detonators or exploders, i.e., explosives which start explosive reactions in the explosives of Group (a).

The characteristic of H.E. is the extreme violence and suddenness of their detonation.

In order to make them instantly pass from a solid or liquid form to gas, they require a detonator or exploder, which applies a violent shock to them and breaks down the chemical structure of the explosive compound, and enables the flame to pass instantaneously throughout the mass of the compound. This explosive is known as detonation.

The composition of H.E. almost without exception is some organic substance, usually some form of carbon combined with nitrogen. Nitrogen, one of the most inert gases known, owes its explosive value to this very inertness; it combines so very reluctantly that on the least provocation—such as shock—the compound of which it forms a part instantly breaks up into gas, giving the enormous expansion needed for explosive effect.

Ammonal. A gray powder. An Austrian explosive,

picric acid plus T.N.T. plus aluminum powder plus nitrate of ammonia plus carbon.

A very safe explosive—will not detonate when struck by rifle bullet, but is very hygroscopic (collects moisture) and when in this condition is liable not to detonate.

Ballistite. Consists of guncotton plus camphor or vaseline. Invented by Nobel in 1888.

Cordite. Consists of nitro-glycerine 55 parts, plus guncotton 37 parts, plus vaseline 5 parts, plus acetone to harden, invented by Sir W. Abel.

Benzol. Or Benzine, used extensively as a motor fuel contains a fair percentage of toluene. (See T.N.T.)

Coal Tar. When subjected to fractional and low-temperature distillation produces many by-products valuable in the making of H.E. These distillations give off "light" and "heavy" oils of coal tar.

Donnerite. High explosive employed by German army in grenades.

Dynamite. See Nitro-glycerine.

Fulminate of Mercury. See Mercury.

Guncotton, or nitro-cellulose consists of cotton waste, purified, dried, and heated with mixture of concentrated nitric and sulphuric acid. Washed and reduced to a pulp and moulded into 1-oz. primers and 15-oz. slabs for service use. Is considered inferior to lyddite.

Size of wet slab of G.C., $6 \times 3 \times 1\frac{3}{8}$ in.

Wet guncotton will not explode if hit by a bullet.

Wet guncotton can be sawn by a wet saw.

Requires dry primer, detonator and fuse to explode.

Dry guncotton will explode if hit by a bullet.

Dry primer of guncotton 1.35 in. diam., 1.15 in. diam. at ends, and 1.25 in. high.

Strength, $2\frac{1}{2}$ times stronger than gunpowder, unconfined.

Strength, 7 to 8 times stronger than gunpowder, confined.

Invented by Schombein in 1846.

Gunpowder. A mechanical mixture.

Saltpeter 75 per cent, plus charcoal 15 per cent, plus sulphur 10 per cent. Rate of burning depends upon firmness of powder.

Lyddite, or picric acid. Consists of melted and solidified picric acid. Vaseline is used to melt it. (See Picric Acid.)

Mercury Fulminate. Is made by dissolving three parts mercury in 36 parts nitric acid, keeping mixture at low temperature, and when dissolved adding 17 parts of alcohol.

A small quantity of F. of M. placed on top of T.N.T. forms an excellent detonating mixture. A great many German detonators consist of this. Discovered by Howard in 1800.

Melinite. A French H.E., very similar to lyddite. Is picric acid mixed with collodion. Introduced by Eugene Turpin.

Nitro-glycerine. Is produced by the action of nitric acid and sulphuric acid on glycerine. Invented in 1847. When pure is a colorless liquid. Explodes when heated to about 360° F.

N.G. in liquid form too dangerous to be used in practice. Was absorbed in porous solid by Nobel in 1867 as dynamite. Porous solid used either **kiesulguhr** or **fullers' earth** used in percussion caps.

Relative strength......	150 equals maximum
Blasting glycerine	150
Gelatine dynamite.....	130
Gelignite	110
Dynamite............	100
Carbonite...........	55

Picric acid. A yellow crystalline prepared from coal tar. A by-product of gas manufacture. The "heavy oil" of coal tar is boiled and chemically treated, resulting in phenol or carbolic acid, which separates from it.   Carbolic acid is boiled sulphuric acid, and nitric acid is carefully added, resulting in picric acid.

It is a very safe explosive and very powerful.   Its chief fault is that it forms "picrates" with metals or acid salts, some of which are more sensitive to disturbing influences than the acid itself.   To overcome this the inside of all shells are varnished.

Pressure of picric acid equals 135,820 lb. on the square inch.

Shimose.   Japanese H.E.   Similar to lyddite.

T.N.T., or tri-nitro-toluene or Toluol, largely used in German army and navy.   Is produced by heating toluene with mixture of nitric and sulphuric acid.

Less powerful than lyddite, but is more stable and does not form "picrates" and is not affected by water or air.   Will not explode if hit by a bullet.

Pressure T.N.T. equal to 119,000 lbs. per square inch.

Tolite.   French name for T.N.T.

Trilite.   Spanish name for T.N.T.

Trotyl.   German name for T.N.T.

Toluene, or Toluol.   Experiments made in 1899 at Karlsruhe produced about seven pints of toluene from one ton of coal.   The modern process of low-temperature distillation of coal, however, greatly increases quantity that can be obtained from each ton.

Is an aromatic colorless liquid hydrocarbon.

Turpinite.   French H.E. similar to Melinite.

Tetryl.   A coal tar product containing more nitrogen than T.N.T. of lyddite.   When mixed with a lead oxide it makes a less sensitive and safer preparation than fulminate of mercury for detonators.

FUSES

SERVICE FUSE

No. 11 Safety or Time Fuse

Description. Color, black. Smooth surface.
Time of Burning. One foot in thirty seconds.
Composition. Train of slow match inside a wrapping of hemp or flax, covered by layer of gutta-percha, surrounded by binding of black waterproof tape.

INSTANTANEOUS OR QUICK FUSE

Color, red. Ribbed surface.
Time of Burning. Eighty feet per second.
Composition. Same as service fuse, except that it contains quick match in place of slow match.
Caution. Instantaneous fuse must never be stored alongside safety fuse.

DETONATORS

SERVICE

No. 8 Mark VII

Description. Copper tube open at one end painted red, marked on white label, No. 8. M.K. VII containing 32 grs. fulminate of mercury.

COMMERCIAL (Long)
COMMERCIAL (Short)

Description. Copper tube, open one end, containing 25 grs. fulminate of mercury.

EXPLODERS

SERVICE

Guncotton. One-oz. primer, 15-oz. slab. See Explosives, Guncotton.

No. 2 Detonator for Hand Grenade. Consists of brass tube (detonator holder) with flat screw head. The other end is fitted with a cavity which carries N.G. percussion cap. A commercial detonator open end toward the screw head is placed inside, its open end closed with a wooden plug; the closed end is pierced with four flash holes to enable flash from percussion cap to communicate with F. of M. in detonator. A brass screw in head of detonator holder closes detonator tube.

This detonator has three screw threads.

No. 3 Detonator. See description of No. 2. This detonator is $\frac{1}{4}$ in. longer than No. 2, and has two screw threads.

PATENT LIGHTERS

Nobel Lighter. (See Plates 8 and 9.) The lighter is made up of two cardboard tubes, one fitting over the other; inside the end of the larger tube is a small brass cap containing friction composition. At the top of the smaller tube are two friction points. These points are held about $\frac{1}{4}$ in. from the cap containing friction composition, by a safety pin passing through both tubes. At the other end of the smaller tube is a small copper band into which the fuse can be crimped. A narrow band of waterproof tape with a loose end is glued around the joint of the two tubes to keep out moisture.

To Assemble. Insert fuse into lighter, fasten by crimping, and insert other end of fuse into detonator. The joints at lighter and detonator should be waxed to make it damp-proof and flash-proof.

Brock Lighter. See Grenade Hand. Consists of a small cardboard cup filled with friction composition, covered with waterproof paper. The latter can be torn off by pulling a small tag which is left free.

Grenades with fuses are so arranged (with sufficient length of fuse) to explode from 3 to 5 seconds after being ignited and thrown, giving the thrower plenty of time (when throwing from a trench) to bend down safe. Grenades, without fuses (but with detonators only) will explode on impact; for instance, in Grenade No. 1, Mark I, it is obvious when instructions (see p. 2, Grenade 1) are carried out, and grenade is thrown, that the steel needle will be driven into the detonator and exploded.

In Grenade No. 3, Mark I, when safety pin is removed and releasing socket slipped back, the wind vane revolves backward (during the passage through the air) until far enough to allow the retaining bolt to fall out. This leaves nothing between the firing needle and detonator cap except a very thin spiral spring which is only strong enough to hold the weight of the needle pellet until the shock of impact when the grenade explodes.

In Grenade No. 20 releasing collar slips back on the rifle being fired.

In Grenade No. 5, Mark I. On this grenade being thrown the pressure of the fingers being released the striking lever flies outward by the pressure of the powerful spring, releasing the shoulder of the firing striker which is driven on to the fuse and explodes in $4\frac{1}{2}$ seconds.

All other grenades, see pages opposite plates.

THROWING

Hand grenades are held firmly in the hand behind the thrower, the arm is brought quickly upward with a sweeping movement (the arm straight all the time), the grenade will be let go when the hand is above the thrower's head, and should describe a semicircle in its flight.

Hand grenades can be thrown from 30 to 50 yards, rifle grenades from 200 to 400 yards.

Attacks should be practiced with dummy and deteriorated grenades, i.e., grenades with only a detonator and no explosive, etc.

Confidence and knowledge of grenades should be gained by students handling, stripping and assembling all types and handling fuses and detonators, as often as possible.

The importance of grenade work cannot be over-estimated and one can imagine numberless cases when a grenade is more useful than any other weapon. For instance, in street fighting a number of the enemy are holding a house and firing from an upper window commanding the main approach. You cannot get at them with a rifle, but it might be comparatively easy for one or two men to get along to the house by back ways, using the other houses for shelter and throw a grenade through the window, killing everyone in the room.